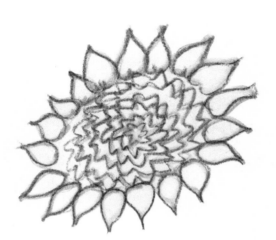

The Waldorf Book of Breads

The
Waldorf
Book of Breads

Collected by Marsha Post
Illustrated by Jo Valens
Edited and Introduced by Winslow Eliot

STEINERBOOKS

Copyright by SteinerBooks 2009

Illustrations copyright by Jo Valens 2009

Published by SteinerBooks
610 Main Street
Great Barrington, Massachusetts 01230

www.steinerbooks.com

Library of Congress Cataloging-in-Publication Data

Post, Marsha.
  The Waldorf book of breads / collected by Marsha Post;
illustrated by Jo
Valens ; edited and introduced by Winslow Eliot.
     p. cm.
  Includes index.
    ISBN 978-0-88010-703-7
    1. Bread. I. Eliot, Winslow. II. Pleasant Ridge Waldorf School (Viroqua,
Wis.) III. Title.
    TX769.P657 2009
    641.8'15--dc22

                              2009042304

Printed in the United States of America

Contents

Acknowedgements

For generations recipes have been exchanged at reunions, family dinners, potlucks, or wherever home-cooked food was being served. It was always the mark of a good cook to be asked for a recipe, and that of a gracious person to share it.

SteinerBooks would like to thank all of you—teachers, parents, staff, and friends of the Waldorf movement—who have joined this tradition by passing along your favorite bread recipes to all of us. Many of your recipes were handed down from mothers, aunts, and grandmothers. And who knows from whom they received them?

Very special thanks goes to Carolina Gordon, baker at the Hawthorne Valley Bakery, for her helpful insights and wisdom.

Introduction

Why bake your own bread?

When I was growing up my mother, who read more books about baking bread than anyone I know, used to talk to us about something she called "the initiation of the daily life." In her view, the most spiritual activity was often the most mundane and, likewise, mundane necessities were often the most spiritual — when paid proper attention. In our family, making bread epitomized this. Her words, along with the smell of warming yeast and baking bread, are linked in my childhood memories.

It was only as my children were growing up that I began to understand what she meant. When our family all together mixed, stirred, kneaded, waited with happy anticipation, and, best of all, tasted a hot, fresh loaf of bread, we were undergoing the initiation of the daily life. Decision, attention, hard work, patience, letting go, baking, and celebration could all be harvested in a single afternoon devoted to baking bread.

Bread — in one form or another — is eaten by people of every race, culture, and religion. It is used ritualistically and symbolically in more places than any other food, and it is also a daily staple of many peoples' diet.

There is great joy and a sense of accomplishment in making bread. The process of kneading, the delightful smell as it is baking, the delicious taste of fresh bread, all nourish not just our hungry bellies, but our souls as well.

The activity itself is not the only reason for baking your own bread. Also important is the quality of the organic — preferably bio-dynamic — ingredients you are able to use. The nutritional value of homemade bread far exceeds factory-made. Organic fields are fertilized by naturally occurring substances, creating a soil rich in nutrients. The result is a grain that is wholesome and truly tasty. Even if you make a mistake along the way, when you use the highest quality ingredients the final product will still be delicious. If you want to experiment with other grains or exchange whole wheat flour with organic white flour, then by all means go ahead. When you use your creativity to experiment with recipes, making bread becomes one of the most rewarding activities in your home.

It is our hope that this little book will be a stepping stone to encourage bread baking — and bread eating — so that it re-emerges in our culture as the nourishing blessing it has been for thousands of years.

Winslow Eliot

1

Making Bread

"Matter is never without spirit and spirit never without matter." — Rudolf Steiner

Creating a loaf of bread is one of the simplest and yet most rewarding things you can do with children. In one small loaf you have created an entire world, and children love that! All four elements that are essential to life are inherent in your single loaf of bread: earth in the salt mineral and the grain; water; air in the carbohydrates and yeast (as a one-cell organism, yeast cannot exist without air); and fire, which finalizes the process, bringing the loaf to life by baking it.

Making bread is a uniquely human activity. Without you as the initiator, bread would never exist. Human hands are needed to guide the process, as well as human attention, patience, and intuition. Each time you take your loaf to the next stage, you are bringing it into a higher level of existence.

So, it is important to put a lot of consciousness into making bread, especially when you are baking with children. Be attentive, serious, joyful at each step along the way—when you're tiptoeing away to let the bread do its thing or when you're actively engaging in punching it down for its next kneading. In this way, you'll discover how important the human touch is in making bread. You can actually begin to sense timing, readiness, what the bread requires next.

Focus only on what you are doing. Try to visualize what is happening during the mixing, and kneading, and fermentation processes. Imagine the chaos of separation and the harmony of unity at each stage—breathing in and breathing out. Even without speaking this out loud, children will pick up on your attentiveness and understand intuitively the magical alchemical activity you are involved in.

As you work with bread in this way, you'll become aware of the four life forces that are at work: the physical ingredients, the etheric activity of kneading, the soul process during the time of fermentation, and the ego that emerges from you, the human being who creates the loaf.

"My experience over all these years is that the human touch is the most important aspect of making bread," says Hawthorne Valley Farm baker Carolina Gordon. "The hands are shaping the bread—and kneading the bread. We make all the bread by hand. It's more work, but I like the fact that everyone is taking part in every aspect. It's like being an artist. And you can always tell a loaf made by someone who is still learning, because it is still so much a part of that person. Only when it becomes itself does it truly become a great loaf of bread. It's like listening to a great concerto: if a musician is a real artist you don't hear how good the musician is – you hear the actual music."

The History of Bread

The humble food called grain has been a principal source of nutrition for humans from earliest recorded history. It is even referred to in an ancient Sumerian creation myth, and anthropologists have discovered seeds of wheat and tools for grinding them that are over 8,000 years old.

There are seven major grains, and each emerged from a different part of the globe: wheat, oats, rye, barley in Europe; corn in the Americas; rice in Asia; and millet in Africa. For thousands of years people used mortars to powder all these grains (except for rice) in order to make flat breads. Wheat and, to a lesser extent, rye are the only grains that can be used to make leavened bread.

According to legend, the first leavened loaf of bread occurred accidently. Sometime around three thousand years ago, an Egyptian baking apprentice forgot to bake a flat bread before leaving the bakery. Over the next days, wild air-borne yeast spores permeated the flatbread, causing it to swell as it broke down into complex carbohydrates, to simple carbs, then to carbon dioxide and alcohol. The first leavened loaf of bread was created! The high gluten content of the wheat heightened this leavening process, and wheat quickly became the most popular grain, for those who could afford it.

The shift in human consciousness that occurred around this time is reflected in this change from two-dimensional flatbread to three-dimensional loaves. Bread became a whole meal in and of itself. The only required ingredients were wheat, water, salt, and yeast. Not only could you survive on its rich nutrients, but you could easily carry it around with you: the hard crust on the outside protected the soft tasty "crumb" inside.

A love for bread flourished in the centuries that followed. In ancient Greece, friendly competitions were held between city-states to see which produced the best bread. The first known Bakers Guild was formed in Rome about the year 168 BCE. All through ancient times bread and bakers were held in the highest respect.

Around 1200 CE, England created legislation so that bakers could not sell loaves that did not conform to the weights that were required by law. As a result of the "bread trials" in England in 1266, bakers were ordered to mark each loaf so a dishonest baker could be tracked down and prosecuted. The bakers' marks were among the first known "trademarks."

Mills that ground the grain to a fine flour were powered by wind or water until the middle of the nineteenth century, when an enterprising Swiss engineer designed the steam-driven "reduction roller-milling system" made of steel rollers. Hugely successful, this invention enabled the cheap and rapid production of white bread flour for the first time.

Unfortunately, this innovation meant that most of the nutrition in bread was lost. This is because the wheat germ, or embryo, is enhanced by no less than seven layers of complex carbohydrates, all of which provide essential nutrients and vitamins. These delicate, nutritious layers are called, poetically, in German "silber häutchen"; literally, the "silver lining." The outer shell holds the important bran and fiber. Even processing regular whole wheat flour removes this outer shell, unless the whole grain is milled. This is one reason why it is so important to use whole grains whenever possible when you are baking bread!

Back to Scratch

By Marsha Post

One of my most vivid memories of childhood was coming home from school every Wednesday afternoon. The minute I opened the back porch door I was met with the aroma of baked bread, fresh from the oven. Mom was usually just rubbing the tops of the loaves with homemade butter when I walked in. It was hard to wait until it had cooled enough, so I could have a slice. She baked five loaves of bread every week, and always from scratch; in those days there was no other way to bake your own bread.

Years later, however, someone invented the automatic bread machine. Mom thought it would be great to have such a time-saving device. I bought her one, and she did not waste any time trying it out. She followed the instructions exactly as they were given and selected the proper settings for the bread to bake. Although I was now an adult, it was still hard to wait for my slice of buttered bread.

But it was not to be. The loaf turned out to be about the same shape and weight of a thick brick.

There was nothing to do but toss it out. Mom assured me that it would not go completely to waste because the big old mother raccoon and her babies that lived in the cornfield would eat it. She broke it into three chunks and tossed them out by the edge of the field. Sure enough, toward evening a huge raccoon came out and carried off a chunk. But the next morning that chunk of bread was again lying with the others. The raccoon had brought it back!

Now, in Mom's defense, the machine did have a defect. I bought her a new one, and she used it once or twice, but then never again. After the raccoon incident, she decided to go back to baking from scratch!

Wheat Breads

Wheat is officially classified as a grass, and yet no one has yet discovered the wild form of grass from which wheat, as we know it today, originally came. Vestiges of the first cultivated wheat have been found in the great fertile valley of Mesopotamia, the "cradle of civilization."

Like most wild grass, cereal blossoms bear both male and female elements. The young seeds are provided with a store of food to ensure their support during the period of germination, and it is from this store that our bread is made.

If you look closely at a wheat grain it looks like a seed, but a closer examination reveals that it is a true fruit. You'll find a fruit-leaf with its edges rolled over and grown together, and a furrow running along its length.

Whole wheat flour is rich in complex carbohydrates, which provide a source of time-released energy. It also provides protein for growth, essential B vitamins for a sound nervous system and digestion, and important minerals like iron, thiamin, niacin, riboflavin, and calcium, which ensure healthy blood and strong bones and teeth.

An amazing source of nourishment!

Please note: Although not always indicated in the individual recipes, we hope you will be able to use flours from bio-dynamically, or at least organically, grown grains. You may also substitute whole grain flour where it calls for white flour, but you may need to experiment with quantities and baking times.

Four-Seeded Bread

This is the recipe for my most popular bread sold at the Viroqua Farmer's Market.

5 T. baking yeast
1/4 cup vegetable oil
1/2 cup non-instant organic milk powder
1/4 cup blackstrap molasses
8 cups warm water (approximately 100°)
3 T. salt
2 cups rolled oats
4 cups Guisto's ultimate performer whole wheat flour
High-gluten white flour, enough for kneadable dough
1 cup sunflower seeds
1/4 cup flax seeds
1/2 cup millet
1/2 cup sesame seeds

Place yeast, oil, milk powder, and molasses in warm water, stir and let sit for 5 minutes. Stir in oats and 4 cups whole wheat flour and salt, let sit 5 minutes. Add seeds and high-gluten flour. Knead well. Let rise, till it doubles in size. Punch down and let rise 1/2 hour more. Make into 5 loaves. Let rise until doubled.

Bake in a preheated oven at 400° for 40 to 45 minutes.

Makes 5 loaves.

Carol Willis, Parent
Pleasant Ridge Waldorf School
Viroqua, WI

Greek Sweet Bread

12 cups flour
1-1/2 cups sugar
1 t. salt
2 pkgs. dry yeast
4 cups or more warm water
2 sticks butter, melted
1/2 cup oil
1 egg, beaten (optional)
sesame seeds (optional)

Dissolve the yeast in warm water, and let it stand for a few minutes. Combine the dry ingredients in a large mixing bowl. Add the butter and the yeast mixture, stirring gently to mix. Knead the dough. Keep adding water slowly (up to 2 more cups may be needed). Knead for 15 minutes or more.

Cover dough with a towel and let it rise in a warm place for 1-1/2 to 2 hours, until doubled in size. Knead again while adding oil, a little at a time. Knead thoroughly after each addition. Grease the pans. Divide into loaves. You may also the shape dough into buns or rolls. Allow to rise again until doubled in size, about 1 to 1-1/2 hours.

(*Optional*: Before baking, you can brush the top of the loaves and rolls with beaten egg and sprinkle with sesame seeds.)

Bake at 350° for 50 to 55 minutes.

Makes several loaves, plus a couple of pans of buns.

Originally passed down by
Sophia Chianakas
Peoria, IL

Bread in a Bag

This is a fun children's recipe!

1 cup flour
1 package yeast (about 2 T.)
3 T. sugar
3 T. dry milk
1 t. salt
1 cup hot tap water
3 T. oil
1 cup whole wheat flour
1 cup white flour

Put the 1 cup of flour, the yeast, sugar, milk, and salt in a large sealing bag and shake to mix. Add water and oil. Close bag and squeeze until well-mixed. Add 1 cup whole wheat flour and 1 cup white flour. Close bag and squeeze to mix again. Dough should not stick to the bag. Knead bag 2 to 4 minutes. Let rest 10 minutes. Remove dough from bag and shape into a loaf. Place in a greased pan. Allow to rise until double in size.

Bake at 375° for 25 minutes.

MAKES 1 LOAF.

Vicky Eiben, Spanish Teacher
Pleasant Ridge Waldorf School
Viroqua, WI

Homemade Bread in a Pot

3 cups bread flour
1/4 t. instant dry yeast
1 1/4 t. salt
3 t. gluten (*optional* – gives a chewy texture)
1 5/8 cups water

In a large bowl combine flour, yeast, salt, and the optional gluten. Add the water and stir until blended. The dough will look rough and will be sticky. Cover the bowl with a lid or with plastic wrap and let the dough rest for at least 12 hours, preferably 18 hours, at a warm room temperature of 70°. The dough is ready when the surface is dotted with bubbles.

With the dough still in the large bowl, lightly dust the top of the bubbly dough with flour and stir into a ball. Let this ball of dough rest for 15 minutes.

Using just enough flour to keep the dough from sticking to the work surface or to your fingers, put the dough onto the work surface (a wooden cutting board or breadboard dusted with flour), and gently knead into a round ball. Lightly dust the ball of dough with flour and place it onto a generously floured cotton cloth. Place another generously floured cotton cloth on top of the dough ball and let it rest for 2 hours. (It is very important that the cotton cloths are highly floured so the dough does not stick to them. Otherwise, the dough will tear and not puff up. I prefer to cover the dough ball with wax paper.)

At least 1/2 hour before the dough is ready, preheat the oven to 450°. Put a 6 to 8 quart, heavy, covered pot (cast iron, enamel, Pyrex, or ceramic) in the oven as it heats. When the dough is ready, carefully remove the covered pot from the oven. Slide your hand under the towel and turn the dough over into the hot pan. Gently shake the pan to even the dough in the pan, put the cover back on, and place it in the oven.

Bake for 30 minutes with the lid on. Then remove the lid, lower the temperature to 415° and bake an additional 15 to 30 minutes, until the loaf is beautifully browned.

Cool on a rack. The bread can be sliced in about 3 hours.

MAKES ONE 1-1/2 POUND LOAF.

Gloria Autrey
Ghent, NY

Kindergarten Classroom Bread

This recipe is simple and easy to prepare and adapt for the classroom baking needs. My colleague and mentor Ellen McDermott gave this recipe to me at the Rudolf Steiner School when I was a beginning kindergarten teacher, and I have always used it in my classroom.

I always found it successful, unless I forgot the salt, which happened on occasion and usually meant we would have another opportunity to bake that week. The children loved it when I forgot the salt, because they absolutely loved to bake!

2 pkgs. (2 T.) yeast
2-1/2 cups warm water
3 T. oil
2 t. salt
3 T. honey
3 cups whole wheat flour
3 cups white flour

Prepare the yeast by mixing it with the warm water. Make a "sponge" (a bowl of warm, fermented batter) by combining the oil, salt, and honey with the yeast and 1 cup of the flour. When the sponge is growing begin adding 4 cups of flour.

Sprinkle some flour onto a board, turn the dough onto the board, and knead in the rest of the flour (the dough may be sticky at first). Knead until the dough is damp but not sticky. Let the dough rest while you put on the children's aprons.

Give each child a bit of flour to rub into their hands and about a tablespoon of flour to spread onto the surface of the table. Then give each child a handful of dough that has been dipped into a bowl of flour and let them form rolls. The dough can also be formed into loaves.

Bake in preheated oven at 350° for about 45 minutes, until the crust is golden brown.

MAKES MANY ROLLS OR ABOUT 3 LOAVES.

Cynthia Lang, Remedial Teacher
New York, NY

Quick Brown Bread

1 egg, beaten
1/2 cup molasses
1 cup buttermilk
1/4 cup oil or melted shortening
2 cups wheat flour, sifted
1/2 t. soda
1 t. baking powder
1 t. salt
1/2 cup seedless raisins

Preheat the oven to 350°.

Beat the egg and add the molasses, buttermilk, and oil.

Sift the flour. Add the soda, baking powder, and salt to the flour. Sift this dry mixture into the wet mixture. Add the raisins and mix all together quickly.

Place in a bread pan and bake for 45 minutes.

MAKES ONE LOAF.

Marsha Post
Philmont, NY

Quick Bread Loaves

This is the bread I make when I come home from school in the afternoon and want warm bread for supper. If I get home by 3:30, the bread is ready around 6 p.m. It also makes great pizza dough, and for that it doesn't need to rise more than an hour or so.

2 cups warm water
1 T. active dry yeast
1 T. sugar or honey
4 cups unbleached flour
2 t. salt

Combine water, yeast, and sugar or honey in a large bowl. Let sit for 3 to 5 minutes, until yeast is beginning to foam. Add flour and salt. Stir until all ingredients are well mixed. Dough should be sticky, but still move away from the sides of the bowl. If needed, add 1/4 to 1/2 cup of flour. Cover dough and let sit for 1-1/2 to 2 hours. Oil your hands lightly, so that you can work with the dough. Divide dough into two parts and shape into long loaves. Place on an oiled cookie sheet. (Some people use cornmeal, but I never seem to have it when I need it.)

Preheat oven to 400°.

Let loaves rise while oven is preheating, 15 to 20 minutes. Place sheet in the center of oven and bake for 10 minutes. Reduce heat to 350° and bake for an additional 25 to 30 minutes, until crust is golden brown.

For a harder crust, put a cookie sheet on a rack right underneath the loaves. Put 4 to 5 ice cubes on the tray when the bread goes in the oven. Add more ice at 10 to 15 minute intervals, until the bread is done.

MAKES 2 LOAVES.

Maureen Karlstad, Alumni Parent and Class Teacher
Pleasant Ridge Waldorf School
Viroqua, WI

Whole Wheat Bread 1

3 cups whole wheat flour
1-1/2 T. sugar
2 pkgs. active dry yeast
2 T. melted butter
1-1/4 cups water (room temperature)

Preheat oven to 450°. Preheat a screen wire or a baking stone or pizza stone (baking or pizza stone will require about 40 to 45 minutes to preheat).

Combine dry ingredients in a large bowl. Add the melted butter and water. Mix by hand, or at a low speed if using a mixer. Knead until the dough is smooth. Add more flour or water as needed. The dough should be somewhat tacky, yet not sticky. Place the dough into an oiled bowl and turn the dough to coat it with oil. Cover and allow it to rise until double in size.

Punch down the dough. Let rise again until double in size. Form into loaves and place on the baking stone.

Bake for about 45 minutes, until golden brown (should sound hollow when tapped).

MAKES 2 LOAVES.

Anonymous

Whole Wheat Bread 2

1-1/2 cups warm milk
1 pkg. dry yeast
1/2 T. brown sugar
4 to 5 cups whole wheat flour
1/4 cup brown sugar
1-1/4 t. salt
1/4 cup oil of your choice

Dissolve the 1/2 tablespoon brown sugar in the warm milk. Add the yeast and let the mixture stand.

Sift the flour and return the bran siftings to the flour. Combine 3 cups of this flour with the remaining brown sugar and salt.

Stir the yeast and milk mixture to dissolve the yeast. Add half of the flour mixture to the liquid mixture. Mix thoroughly. Add the oil, mixing well again.

Add the rest of the dry mixture, about 1/2 cup at a time, mixing well each time. Add more flour to the mixture as needed, making a stiff dough (could take up to 1 more cup). When the dough can no longer be stirred with a spoon, turn it out onto a floured breadboard. Knead in more flour until it is firm, and yet still light (could take an additional half cup or so of flour).

Place the dough in a large greased bowl, turning the dough to coat it lightly with oil. Cover the bowl and let it stand in a warm place for about 1 hour. You can place it in an oven set at 90° for this purpose.

Put the dough back onto the breadboard, punch it down, and knead well. Divide and shape the dough into two loaves and place in buttered bread pans (preferably glass). Again cover the bread and let it rise for another 1/2 hour in the warm oven.

Remove the loaves from the oven and warm the oven to 400°. Bake the bread at 400° for 15 minutes. Then lower the temperature to 350° and bake for another 30 minutes.

Turn the loaves out onto wire racks to cool. Butter the top of each loaf.

MAKES 2 LOAVES.

Marsha Post
Philmont, NY

Whole Wheat Bread 3

1 pkg. dry yeast
1/4 cup warm water
1 egg (large), beaten
1/4 cup (1 stick) butter, melted
2-1/2 cups lukewarm water
1 1/2 t. salt
1/4 to 1/2 cup sugar (or honey)
4 cups whole wheat flour
4 cups all-purpose flour

Add dry yeast to 1/4 cup warm water in a large bowl and let it dissolve, without stirring.

Add the egg, butter, lukewarm water, salt, and sugar (honey) to the yeast mixture. Add all of the flour, mixing it in a little at a time.

Turn the dough out onto a floured counter or breadboard. Knead until the dough is smooth and elastic (about 10 minutes). Add water or flour as needed, so the dough does not become either sticky or too dry.

Place the dough into a large, lightly greased bowl. Turn the dough over, in order to grease all the surfaces. Cover the bowl with a clean cloth and let the dough rise in a warm place. Allow it to double in size.

Punch the dough down and turn it again in the bowl. Knead again for a few minutes. (This can be done with the dough still in the bowl.)

Place the dough in greased loaf pans, cover, and allow it to rise again until almost doubled. Preheat the oven at this time to 350°.

Bake approximately 45 minutes, until the crust is golden brown. Remove from the oven and place on a rack to cool.

MAKES 3 LOAVES.

Anonymous

Simple Whole Wheat Rolls

2 T. honey
3 cups warm water
2 T. yeast
3 T. oil
8 cups whole wheat flour

Mix honey, water, and yeast. Stir in the oil and flour. Knead the dough and form into a dozen small rolls. Let the rolls rise for approximately 30 minutes. Bake at 325° for 20 minutes.

When you're making bread you need a little sugar to give the yeast pasture on which to graze, but remember that you can always use real raw sugar or honey instead of white sugar in any bread recipe.

Carolina Gordon
Hawthorne Valley Bakery
Ghent, NY

11

Quotes about Bread

"When we cast our bread upon the waters, we can presume that someone downstream whose face we will never know will benefit from our action, as we who are downstream from another will profit from that grantor's gift." *Maya Angelo*

"Acorns were good till bread was found." **Francis Bacon**

"Bread is the king of the table and all else is merely the court that surrounds the king. The countries are the soup, the meat, the vegetables, the salad, but bread is king." **Louis Bromfield**

"Good bread is the most fundamentally satisfying of all foods; and good bread with fresh butter, the greatest of feasts." **James Beard**

"If thou tastest a crust of bread, thou tastest all the stars and all the heavens." **Robert Browning**

"Without bread all is misery." **William Cobbett**

"With bread all sorrows are less." **Sancho Panza** in "Don Quixote" by Miguel de Cervantes

"There are people in the world so hungry, that God cannot appear to them except in the form of bread." *Mahatma Gandhi*

Spelt Breads

Tasty and nutritious, spelt is one of the oldest grains grown by early farmers, as long ago as 5,000 BCE around the area of Iran. Similar in appearance to wheat, spelt has been called the "grandfather" of wheat. It has a sweet, nutty flavor with a higher protein content than wheat, and the spelt protein is easier to digest. Spelt is also naturally high in fiber, vitamin E and B complex vitamins, and both simple and complex carbohydrates. Spelt contains some gluten, so it cannot be eaten by those who are sensitive to gluten, but some people who are allergic to wheat can still eat spelt.

Spelt has a tough outer hull, or husk, that protects the kernel from fungi diseases, pollutants, and insects, which makes it a favorable grain to grow without using pesticides. The tight husk also helps to maintain nutrients and freshness. Unlike wheat, it has retained many of its original traits and remains highly nutritious and full of flavor. Because of its high water solubility, its nutrients are easily absorbed by the body.

St. Hildegard von Bingen has been one of the greatest advocates for spelt. Born in 1098, she became a nun at the age of sixteen and was renowned as a healer. In 1151, she founded her own convent near Bingen, which became a famous meeting place for all of Europe. Thousands of people visited her for council. St. Hildegard taught that the balance of body, mind, and spirit is key to good health. She believed in the treatment of the entire body, not just the symptom of the illness. Her natural remedies were based on her observations and were shown to her in visions. Her teachings are similar to what is being taught in the natural health world today.

St. Hildegard wrote about spelt: "The spelt is the best of grains. It is rich and nourishing and milder than other grains. It produces a strong body and healthy blood to those who eat it, and it makes the spirit light and cheerful. If someone is ill, boil some spelt, mix it with egg and this will heal the sickness like a fine ointment."

Sweet Peas Preschool Spelt Bread

Our bread recipe is a kind of feel-as-you-go experience. We also found spelt flour to be a good alternative to wheat.

1 T. yeast
1 t. honey
3 cups whole spelt flour
3 cups refined spelt flour
1/2 cup honey
1/2 cup vegetable oil
2 t. salt
2 to 3 cups warm water (enough to make the dough not too sticky)

Mix yeast and honey in a bowl of warm water and let sit until it is bubbly (10 minutes).

Mix all ingredients into the yeast mixture. Knead. Let rise. Poof down. Shape into buns or loaves and let rise again.

Bake rolls at 350° for 20 minutes.
Bake loaves for about 1 hour.

We make the dough and bake the bread the day before we eat it. Then half an hour before lunch, we warm it up at 200°.

MAKES ABOUT ENOUGH FOR 20 HUNGRY CHILDREN.

Johanna J. Hose, Teacher
& Tanya Preston
Sweet Peas Preschool
Kirkland, WA

Corn Breads

Golden-yellow corn, or maize, grows well in warm, sunny climates. It is widely cultivated throughout the world, with the United States producing almost half of the world's harvest. It was first domesticated in Mesoamerica, and then dispersed from there throughout the American continents. In the late fifteenth century after the Europeans made contact with the Americas, corn spread rapidly to the rest of the world.

Corn has a very distinctive form and growth pattern. The stems are erect with many nodes that cast off large flag-like leaves. The ears grow close to the stem directly under the leaves and develop rapidly at about 3 millimeters a day. The ears, the female inflorescences, produce pale yellow silks which are pollinated from the top of the stem — the tassel, an inflorescence of male flowers. Each silk becomes pollinated to produce one kernel of corn. The root system is also different from other grains: the plant's main roots create side roots which expire and are replaced by wreaths which emerge from underground buds on the stalk. Because of its shallow roots, corn is highly susceptible to draught, intolerant of nutrient-deficient soils, and can easily be uprooted by storms.

Native Americans traditionally planted corn in a system called the "Three Sisters" in which corn, beans and squash were planted together on a small "hill": the corn provided support for the beans, the beans provided nitrogen to the soil from the bacteria on its roots, and the squash provided groundcover shade to stop weeds and prevent evaporation. Native Americans dried the corn and ground it into mealcorn. They often ate the corn to gether with beans for strength and stamina.

Modern cornbread is made in much the same way it always has been, although there are many new variations. There are two things to note: 1. Some people are allergic to corn, which contains an undigestible protein that survives cooking. 2. It is important to remember that the cornmeal needs to be quite fresh — if it tastes or smells musty throw it out. Try to buy it from a local health food store if you can.

Corn Bread

1 cup sifted all-purpose flour
1/4 cup sugar
4 t. baking powder
3/4 t. salt
1 cup yellow corn meal
2 eggs
1 cup milk
1/4 cup soft shortening

Sift flour together with sugar, baking powder, and salt. Stir in corn meal. Add eggs, milk, and shortening. Beat with a rotary or electric mixer until just smooth (approximately 1 minute). (It is important not to over-beat the mixture.) Grease a 9"x 9"x 2" baking pan and pour the mixture into it.

Bake at 425° for 12 to 15 minutes.

Velma Post
Rushville, IL

Southern Corn Bread

1 cup corn meal
2 cups milk
2 T. butter
2 eggs, beaten
1 t. baking powder
1 t. salt

Scald the corn meal and milk together. Add the butter. Beat with a mixer until smooth. Cool somewhat and add the beaten eggs, baking powder, and salt.

Place in an 8-inch square pan.

Bake at 425° for 20 to 25 minutes.

Anonymous

New Mexican Corn Bread

6 cups milk
1 can chipolte chilies in adobo sauce
8 cups cornmeal
4 t. soda
2 t. salt
8 eggs
2 cups oil
8 cups creamed corn
8 cups grated pepper jack and white cheddar cheese

Blend milk in a blender with the chilies. In a large bowl mix cornmeal, soda, and salt. Add eggs, oil, creamed corn, and milk mixture. Mix well. Pour half the batter into 4 large, well-buttered pans. Sprinkle cheese over the top of the batter, add the rest of the batter on top of the cheese. The cheese doesn't have to be completely covered.

Bake at 400° for 40 minutes.

MAKES ABOUT 96 (3"x 3") PIECES.

SERVING SUGGESTION:
James Hallberg, another parent at the school and the hot-lunch coordinator, suggests serving honey-butter with the cornbread."The children say, 'Give me as much as is legally allowed!'—which I gladly oblige."

Set some butter out until it is pliable. In a mixing bowl, combine the butter and enough honey to taste. Mush with a potato masher for quickest results.

Janelle Prine, Alumni Parent
Pleasant Ridge Waldorf School
Viroqua, WI

Blue Corn Bread

Use 5 cups total of the following flours:
1 to 2 cups whole-wheat pastry or unbleached
white flour
(For instance: 4 cups cornmeal and 1 cup flour
or 3 cups cornmeal and 2 cups flour)
5 t. baking powder
1/2 to 1 t. salt
3 cups milk (try buttermilk or 1/2 cup
powdered milk in the flour and add water)
3 to 5 cups blue cornmeal
2 eggs
1/2 cup oil

Sift flour, baking powder, salt, and powdered
milk if you are using it. Stir in cornmeal. Make
a well in the flour and put eggs and oil in it.
Mix with a fork. Add liquid. Gradually stir
in flour from the edges. Put the batter in a
greased pan and bake for about 20 minutes.

Emily Bunting, Former parent and
Kindergarten Aide
Pleasant Ridge Waldorf School
Viroqua, WI

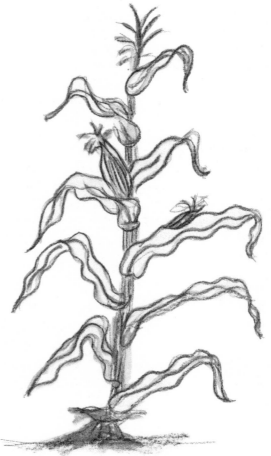

Quotes about Bread

"Bread, milk and butter are of venerable antiquity. They taste of the morning of the world." **Leigh Hunt**

"Love doesn't just sit there, like a stone; it has to be made, like bread, remade all the time, made new." **Ursula K. LeGuin**

"Bread deals with living things, with giving life, with growth, with the seed, the grain that nurtures. It's not coincidence that we say bread is the staff of life." **Lionel Poilâne**

"Were we directed from Washington when to sow and when to reap, we should soon want bread." **Thomas Jefferson**

"Bread is like dresses, hats and shoes—in other words, essential!" **Emily Post**

"Bread and water—these are the things nature requires. For such things no man is too poor, and whosoever can limit his desire to them alone can rival Jupiter for happiness." **Seneca**

"We have learned to see in bread an instrument of community between men—the flavor of bread shared has no equal." **Antoine de Saint-Exupery**

Rye Bread

Rye, a member of the wheat tribe (Triticeae), is closely related to both barley and wheat. It tends to grow in sandy, poor soil and thrives in the cool air of Central and Northern Europe and Russia, but it is less important as a grain crop in other parts of the world. Strong and robust, the kernel is long and gray-bluish. From sowing till harvesting takes twelve whole months. Though archaeological evidence shows that rye was cultivated by the Romans along the Danube and in the British Isles, it does not seem to have been held in high regard as a food. Pliny the Elder dismissed rye as "a very poor food, it only serves to avert starvation." Even mixing it with wheat to lessen its bitter taste did not make it popular with Pliny —"even then it is most unpleasant to the stomach." Personal taste aside, among the benefits of eating rye are said to include strengthening the immune system, increased energy, and relief from allergies.

It is especially good for the liver because of its high kalium content.

Rye is not an easy bread to make. Rye contains a higher proportion of soluble fiber than wheat, but since it has hardly any gluten, it is difficult to it make into a loaf without sourdough starter. The texture of the dough feels a bit like clay and does not hold together unless it is glued with starter. The original leavened bread was sourdough bread made from rye (see page 47). It is also difficult to make a rye loaf without at least half the flour consisting of wheat. While dense, whole rye bread, including pumpernickel, is the main bread eaten in Northern and Eastern Europe, most rye breads in the United States are made with 90% wheat flour. Rye berries can also be cooked and eaten whole or rolled like oats and made into porridge.

Use rye sparingly in very young children's diets.

Pumpernickel

3 – 3-1/2 cups all-purpose flour
2 cups rye flour
3 pkgs. dry yeast
1 T. caraway seeds
1-1/2 cups warm water (approx. 115°)
1/2 cup light molasses
2 T. oil
1 T. salt
enough cornmeal for sprinkling

Combine and mix well 2 cups of the all-purpose flour, the yeast, and the caraway seeds. Mix the warm water, molasses, oil, and salt. Add this to the flour mixture, and mix at a low speed with an electric mixer for approximately 1/2 minute, scraping the sides of the bowl. Beat the mixture 3 minutes at high speed. Stir in the rye flour and as much of the all-purpose flour as can be mixed in with a spoon (3/4 to 1-1/4 cups).

Turn out onto a floured surface and knead in enough of the remaining all-purpose flour to make a moderately stiff dough that is still smooth and elastic (about 6 to 8 minutes). Shape the dough into a ball. Place in a lightly greased bowl and turn it over once to coat all sides. Cover and let rise until it doubles in size.

Punch the dough down and divide it into 2 pieces. Cover it and let it stand for 10 minutes.

Grease a baking sheet and sprinkle with cornmeal. Shape the dough into two round loaves and place on the baking sheet. Flatten the top of the loaves just slightly with your hand. Cover and let them rise until almost double in size.

Bake in a preheated oven at 350° for 35 to 40 minutes, or until well-browned.

MAKES 2 ROUND LOAVES.

Velma Post
Rushville, IL

Jewish Rye Bread

1/2 cup rye flour
1-1/2 cups of high-gluten bread flour
1 T. caraway seeds
1 cup cold water
1 t. salt
1 cup white bread sourdough starter

Mix sourdough, water, and flour together and knead till it comes off the bowl and is shiny (about six minutes). Sprinkle the salt and caraway seeds over the dough and let the salt hydrate for five to ten minutes. Knead again; add a little water if necessary.

Put into the refrigerator till the next morning; then knead the dough again gently for a few minutes; shape into a loaf and put into an oiled bread pan. The dough should fill the pan to about one third from the top.

Put the pan somewhere about 90° — I put it in the oven with just the light on. The dough needs to be kept moist, so spray a little water or place a moist cotton cloth on top. It should be left in a warm, moist place for about 2 hours or until almost double the size.

Sprinkle caraway seeds on top. Score the dough with a long cut, about half an inch deep; make sure the slit is open on either end. (If you don't do this the heels will be too low and the middle too high.)

Preheat the oven to 450°. If you can, place the loaf on a warm tile in the oven to let it rise, instead of in the bread pan. After ten minutes, turn the oven down to 375°. Bake for 45 minutes. When the loaf is cooled a little you can slice it and freeze it for future use.

Carolina Gordon
Hawthorne Valley Bakery
Ghent, NY

Flat Breads

Flour Tortillas 1

I learned how to make tortillas while I was living in Lincoln, Nebraska, and working with the Mexican American community there. The women I knew made piles of them everyday. It was their staple food; they ate everything with tortillas. One of my favorite meals was scrambled eggs and sausage wrapped up in a warm tortilla—a great breakfast!

2 cups flour (white or whole wheat)
1/2 t. salt
1/2 t. baking powder
1/4 cup oil
1/2 cup warm water
Extra flour for rolling out the tortillas

Mix together flour, salt, baking powder, oil, and warm water until the dough forms. Knead the dough until it is smooth (2 to 3 minutes). Dough should not be sticky. Divide the dough into 12 parts. Form each part into a flat, round piece about 1-1/2 inches in diameter. Let the pieces sit for about 5 minutes to make them easier to roll out. Using a rolling pin, roll the pieces into tortillas about 6 to 7 inches in diameter (sprinkle enough flour on both the rolling pin and the dough to keep the dough from sticking to the rolling pin). Cook the tortillas on a hot, DRY cast iron skillet, lightly browning them on each side. Eat while still warm.

MAKES 12 TORTILLAS.

*Maureen Karlstad, Alumni Parent and
Class Teacher
Pleasant Ridge Waldorf School
Viroqua, WI*

Flour Tortillas 2

3 cups flour
1 T. baking powder
1 t. salt
3 T. vegetable oil
1 cup very hot water

Form a large dough ball; let it rest a few minutes. Grab some dough with your hands and form a small dough ball. Roll round and very flat, one at a time as you are cooking, so the dough doesn't dry out. Cook on an ungreased griddle at medium heat, flip when bubbles form.

*Linda Gambrell, Alumni Parent
Pleasant Ridge Waldorf School
Viroqua, WI*

Flat Bread

1 cup water
2 T. corn oil
1/2 t. salt
3 to 4 cups flour (mix of whole wheat and white)

Preheat the oven to 350°.
Mix all the ingredients together.
Knead the dough lightly and form flattened "rolls."

Bake for 20 minutes.

*Christine Inglis
Great Barrington Rudolf Steiner School
Great Barrington, MA*

21

Pita Bread
(also called Pocket Bread)

Pinch off 1/2 cup of dough made from any good whole wheat bread recipe. Flatten it with your hand, bunch up or pull up the sides, and push it into a half-cup measuring cup. Use your thumb to take off any excess protruding out of the top of the cup. Dump this out onto the counter or breadboard and repeat, until the dough is used up. This procedure assures a uniform size and a smooth surface on the bottom of the dough.

Let the dough rounds rise a bit, but not too long. Roll them out into circles about 1/4 to 1/8 inch thick and about 8 inches in diameter. Let them rise again briefly.

It is nice to bake these pita breads on screen wire or on a hot baking or pizza stone. If you do not have one of these, a baking sheet may be used (allow about 5 minutes for preheating). Spray the stone with a mist of water and wait about 30 seconds.

Place as many rounds of bread on the stone as will fit without touching each other.

Bake the pitas at 450° for 7 minutes. After about 4 minutes, you should be able to see them puffing up. (If you leave the breads in the oven too long, they will not deflate into the flat rounds.)

Repeat until all the breads are baked.

MAKES ABOUT 8 PITAS.

Clopper Almon
Silver Springs, MD

Armenian Thin Bread
(Sesame Seed Crackers)

1/4 cup butter
2 T. honey
1 t. salt
1 T. yeast
1 cup warm water
1 cup whole wheat flour
1-1/2 to 2-1/2 cups unbleached white flour
1/2 cup sesame seeds

Melt butter. Add honey and salt. Proof yeast in water. Cool and combine with butter and honey. Add whole wheat flour, work in sesame seeds. Add the rest of the flour until you achieve bread-like consistency. Let rise until doubled. When doubled, divide into fourths. Roll out to desired thinness without oil or flour. Put on a cookie sheet.

Bake at 350° until done, about 15 to 20 minutes.

Sherry Knapp, Former parent
Pleasant Ridge Waldorf School
Viroqua, WI

Sesame-Oat Crackers

5 cups rolled oats
1 cup flour, rice or wheat
1 t. salt
1/2 cup sesame seeds
1/2 cup oil
1 cup water

Mix dry ingredients in a bowl. Emulsify the oil in water. Cut into dry ingredients. With your fingers, work dough until it is well blended. Roll out and cut into shapes. Sprinkle with salt.

Heat oven to 400°. Reduce heat to 325° for baking. Bake for 25 minutes, or until golden.

Julee Caspers Agar, Former parent and teacher
Pleasant Ridge Waldorf School
Viroqua, WI

Fruit Breads

Apple Bread

2 cups sugar
1 cup oil
3 eggs, beaten
3 cups flour
1 t. salt
1 t. cinnamon
2 t. vanilla
1 t. soda
3 cups grated apples

Mix the sugar, oil, and beaten eggs together in a large mixing bowl.

Add the flour, salt, cinnamon, vanilla, soda, and grated apples.

Pour into 2 greased and floured loaf pans. Sprinkle with sugar.

Bake 1 hour at 325°.

J. Ervin
Rushville, IL

Strawberry Nut Bread

3 cups sifted flour
1 t. soda
1 t. salt
1 T. cinnamon
2 cups sugar
4 eggs, beaten
1-1/4 cups oil
2 cups slice strawberries
1-1/4 cups chopped pecans

Sift all the dry ingredients together into a large mixing bowl. Make a well in the center and add the liquid mixture. Stir just enough to moisten.

Pour into 2 greased 9"x 5"x 3" pans.

Bake in a moderate oven (350°) for 1 hour. Let cool 5 minutes before taking the loaves out of the pans. Finish cooling on wire racks.

Vilma Post
Canton, IL

Banana Bread

1/3 cup vegetable shortening
2 eggs
1 cup rolled oats
1/2 t. soda
1 cup mashed bananas
2/3 cup sugar
1 cup sifted flour
2 t. baking powder
1 t. salt
2/3 cup chopped nuts

Mix the ingredients in the order given above. Put into a greased bread pan.

Bake at 350° for 1 hour.

Virginia Stambaugh
Rushville, IL

Banana Nut Bread

A Parent/Child Program morning favorite!

2 cups whole wheat flour
1 t. baking soda
1/2 cup oil (coconut)
1/2 cup honey
1 grated lemon rind
2 beaten eggs
2 cups ripe banana pulp
1/4 t. salt
1/2 cup chopped nuts (crispy almonds)
1/2 cup raisins (optional)

Sift together flour and baking soda. Blend oil, honey, and lemon rind until nearly smooth. Beat in eggs.

Add sifted ingredients in three parts alternately with banana pulp, beating until smooth after each addition. Fold in chopped nuts. Place in a large, greased loaf pan.

Bake at 350° for 50 minutes, or until a fork or toothpick in the center comes out dry. Cool five minutes before removing from pan.

HINTS:
1. I like to measure out the oil first in a cup. Then measure the honey afterward in the same cup, and it pours right out!
2. Instead of a loaf pan, I recommend a 9"x 13" glass dish. There is a little less baking time, and it is easier to cut and serve.

Sarah Caldwell, Parent,
teacher substitute
Pleasant Ridge Waldorf School
Viroqua, WI

Raisin Cinnamon Bread

1 qt. boiling water
1/3 cup dark syrup
4 t. salt
4 T. shortening
2 T. cinnamon
1 cup raisins
2 cakes compressed yeast
1/2 cup lukewarm water
3 to 4 qt. flour (approximately 9 cups)

Pour boiling water over dark syrup, salt, shortening, cinnamon, and raisins. Let cool to lukewarm (or 80°). Break yeast into lukewarm water and add to the above mixture. Sift the flour and add gradually until the dough is stiff enough to transfer to a breadboard. Knead in flour until the dough does not stick to the board. Knead well (10 to 12 minutes) and place the dough in a greased bowl. Spread some soft shortening over the dough. Let it rise until it doubles in size. Punch it down and let it rise again until it is a little more than double in size. Divide it into 4 parts and shape each part into a loaf. Let rise until they are light.

Bake at 350° for 40 to 50 minutes.

MAKES 4 LOAVES.

Velma Post
Rushville, IL

Festival Breads

Breaking bread is a universal sign of peace. For thousands of years bread has been connected in various ways with religious rites and social covenants.

Hot cross buns commemorate Lent and Good Friday, Greek Easter breads are set with eggs dyed red to denote the blood of Christ, and Jewish families celebrate the coming of the Sabbath with a delicious yeast bread known as Challah.

Traditionally, festival breads are made with special ingredients that have some sort of significance.

Perhaps you'd like to create your own tradition with a holiday or festival recipe that you create yourself.

Harvest Bread

1/2 cup cornmeal
1/2 cup honey
1/4 cup oil
1 T. salt
2 cups boiling water
2 T. yeast
1/2 cup warm water
1 cup rye flour
1 cup whole wheat flour
1 cup toasted sunflower seeds
1/4 cup poppy seeds
3 cups whole wheat flour

Mix together cornmeal, honey, oil, and salt. Pour the boiled water over this mixture; let stand to cool. Dissolve yeast in 1/2 cup warm water and add to the cooled mixture. Add rye flour and 1 cup whole wheat flour, and beat well. Add the seeds, mix well. Finish with adding the rest of whole wheat flour. Let rise, punch down, and divide into two loaves. Let rise until almost double.

Bake at 350° for 45 minutes.

MAKES 2 LOAVES.

Kristy Wiltrout, Parent
Pleasant Ridge Waldorf School
Viroqua, WI

Dragon Bread 1

For Michaelmas, this loaf is a special shape rather than a special recipe. The teachers who make this loaf use their regular bread recipe and then shape the dough as described in these two examples.

1. Create the dragon's head, body, and tail.
2. Use more dough to create lots of spikes!

Nancy Segreto
Green Mountain Waldorf School
Vermont

Harvest Wheat-Sheaf Bread

This is a special shaped loaf rather than a special recipe. Use a regular bread recipe and shape the dough as described below.

Have the children roll the dough into long thin "snakes." Have a few children roll out an extra-long piece of dough.

Arrange all the shorter snakes on a cookie sheet to be the wheat. Use the longest snake to wrap around the wheat and tie it into a bow. Snip the ends of the snakes to make it look like a sheaf of wheat.

Bake at 350° for about 30 minutes, or until done.

Serve on a quite large breadboard with butter and grapes.

Diane Prusha
Great Barrington Rudolf Steiner School

Dragon Bread 2

1. Create the dragon's head, body, and tail.
2. Add almonds for the scales.
3. Use a raisin for the eye and red fruit for fire.

Maryla Sikora
Four Winds School
Illinois

Pumpkin Muffins

2 cups pumpkin
2-2/3 cups flour
1/2 cups ground seeds (raw sunflower, sesame, pumpkin)
4 t. baking powder
1/4 t. baking soda
3 t. cinnamon
1 t. nutmeg
2/3 cup oil
1/2 cup honey
4 T. molasses

Preheat oven to 350°. Oil the muffin pans.

Mix all ingredients until just blended.

Bake for 30 minutes.

Ruth Kasl
Kindergarten Teacher
Susquehanna Waldorf School
Marietta, PA

Santa Lucia Buns

1/4 cup water
2 pkgs. yeast
2 cups warm milk
2 eggs (1 in dough, 1 topping)
1-1/4 cups sugar
8 cups flour
1-1/2 t. salt
2 sticks butter, melted

In a large bowl, combine water and yeast. Allow to become foamy. Mix together all ingredients (1 egg), except the butter. Mix in the butter. Knead the dough for 10 minutes. Let rise for 1 hour. Punch down the dough. Form into figure-eight shapes by first making long, thin ropes with the dough. Then form into a figure-eight shape or an S shape. Brush egg whites on the buns before baking.

Bake at 350° for 20 to 30 minutes.

Kristen Carr
The Waldorf School
Lexington, MA

Sufganiyot (orange flavored donuts)

This is a traditional Chanukah treat in Israel. It is a mitzvah (commandment) to eat oil for Chanukah, and so potato latkes are the usual fare, but I make sufganiyot with my Nursery children. Donuts are typically fried, but this is a baked version for the festival season.

1 juice orange, the juice and zest
1/2 cup oil or margarine (not butter – it burns)
1/2 cup organic sugar (or 1/4 cup maple syrup)
1 T. yeast
2 eggs
3 cups flour (you can mix whole wheat and white)
1/4 t. salt
oil
powdered sugar (optional)

Mix the orange juice, oil, and sugar, and heat it slightly, stirring until sugar dissolves. Cool to lukewarm and add the yeast. Stir until dissolved. Add eggs, flour, zest of the orange, and salt. Mix to form a smooth dough. Knead. If the dough is sticky, add a bit of flour to it or flour your hands.

Cover and let it rise 1/2 hour. With oil on your hands, roll the dough into small balls and place them fairly closely together on baking sheets. Let them rise for 1/2 hour.

Bake at 400° for 10 minutes.

Options: Sprinkle with powdered sugar or maple sugar crystals. Dip them in jam.

MAKES ENOUGH AS SNACKS FOR A LARGE GROUP OF CHILDREN.

Andrea Gambardella,
Sunbridge College
Chestnut Ridge, NY

27

Gingerbread People

1/3 cup butter
2/3 cup honey
2/3 cup molasses
5 cups whole wheat flour
1-1/2 t. baking soda
1/2 t. cloves
1/2 t. cinnamon
3 t. ginger
1 t. salt

Preheat the oven to 350°.

Blend the butter, honey, and molasses.

Sift the dry ingredients.

Add the sifted ingredients to the butter mixture. If the dough is too dry, add a little water or milk until the dough forms a ball.

Chill for 1 hour, if the dough is sticky.

Roll out the dough to 1/4 inch thick. Cut out gingerbread people.

Bake for 8 to 10 minutes.

Kirsten Carr
The Waldorf School
Lexington, MA

Christmas Stollen

8 cups all purpose flour
2 cakes compressed yeast
1-1/2 cups scalded milk, cooled
1/2 cup raisins
1/2 cup slivered almonds
1/2 cup mixture of finely chopped, dried mixed fruit
3/4 cup sugar
1-1/2 cups butter
3 eggs
1/2 t. salt
1 t. lemon rind
2 T. brandy or rum

Preheat oven to 350°.

Sift flour. Crumble yeast into milk and let stand for 10 minutes or until dissolved. Add 1 cup of flour. Permit this to rise in a warm place until doubled in bulk.

Combine raisins, almonds, and mixed dried fruit with a little of the flour. Beat sugar into butter and blend until it is light and creamy. Beat in eggs. Then add salt, lemon rind, and rum or brandy. Add fruit and nut mixture.

Add the risen flour and the remaining flour, and knead the dough until it is smooth and elastic. Permit it to rise until almost double in bulk.

Divide it into 2 loaves on a floured board and shape into oblong loaves. Place the loaves on a cookie sheet and brush with melted butter. Cover the loaves and let them rise until they again almost double.

Bake for about 45 minutes. When they are cool, brush them with lemon glaze. *(See recipe, next page)*

Lemon glaze:
1-1/4 cups confectioner's sugar
1/4 cup fresh lemon juice
1 t. vanilla

Mix ingredients until smooth and spread on top of the cooled stollen.

MAKES 2 LOAVES.

Caroline Geissler
Ghent, NY

Caroline, a graduate of the Rudolf Steiner School in New York City, has been making this lovely stollen for Christmas gifts for teachers of her five children at Hawthorne Valley School for many years.

Irish Soda Bread 1

Dry ingredients:
1-2/3 cups white flour
1/3 cup corn meal
2 T. oat bran
1/4 cup whole wheat flour
3/8 cup sugar
1/2 t. salt
1 t. baking powder
3/4 t. baking soda
1-1/2 t. ground caraway seed

Wet ingredients:
1 egg
1/2 cup yogurt or buttermilk
1/4 cup safflower oil or melted butter

Hold separate:
1/2 cup raisins

Mix the dry ingredients together. Mix the wet ingredients together. Then add the wet mixture to the dry mixture. Knead for 1 minute. Add the 1/2 cup raisins.

Bake at 350° for 45 minutes, or until done.

Madeline Blumbeck
Spring Valley, NY

Irish Soda Bread 2

4 cups sifted flour
1 t. salt
1/4 cup sugar
1 t. baking powder
1/4 cup butter
2 cups raisins
1-1/3 cups buttermilk
1 egg, unbeaten
1 t. baking soda
1 egg yolk or a little cream

Preheat oven to 375°.

Grease a 2-quart casserole dish. Sift flour, salt, sugar, and baking powder together. With a pastry blender, cut in softened butter until mixture is like coarse cornmeal. Stir in the raisins.

In a separate bowl, combine the buttermilk, egg, and baking soda. Then stir into the flour mixture until moistened.

Turn the dough onto a lightly floured board. Knead lightly until smooth. Shape the dough into a ball and place in a casserole dish.

With a sharp knife, make a 4-inch cross, 1/4 inch deep, on top of the ball. Brush with beaten egg yolk or cream.

Bake for 1 hour and 10 minutes.

Kirsten Carr
The Waldorf School
Lexington, MA

Hot Cross Buns

3-1/2 to 4 cups all-purpose flour
2 pkgs. dry yeast
1 t. ground cinnamon
3/4 cup milk
1/2 cup oil
1/3 cup sugar (granulated)
3/4 t. salt
3 eggs
2/3 cup dried currants

1 egg white
1-1/2 cups sifted powdered sugar
1/4 t. vanilla
dash of salt

Preheat oven to 375°.

Combine 1-1/2 cups of the flour, the yeast,
and the cinnamon in a large bowl.
Mix together milk, oil, granulated sugar, and
the 3/4 teaspoon salt. Heat this until just
warm, stirring the whole time. Add this warm
mixture to the flour mixture.

Add the eggs and, using a mixer, beat at a low
speed for 1/2 minute (scrape sides of bowl
constantly), then 3 minutes at high speed. Using a spoon, mix in the currents and as much
of the remaining flour as you can.

Turn the dough out onto a floured bread board
and knead as much of the remaining flour
into it as is necessary to make a dough that is
moderately soft, smooth, and elastic. Form a
round ball with the dough and turn it over in a
greased bowl to coat all sides. Cover it and let
it stand in a warm spot until it doubles in size.

Punch the dough down and turn it out onto
a floured breadboard. Cover it and allow to
stand for about 10 minutes.

Grease a baking sheet. Divide the dough into
18 pieces, forming them into balls, and place
them on the greased baking sheet. Do not
place them too close together. They should be
about 1-1/2 inches apart. Cover them and let
them rise again until almost double.

Use a very sharp knife to cut a cross in the top
of each bun. Using a pastry brush, apply some
of the egg white to the tops of the buns. Save
the remainder of the egg white.

Bake at 375° for 12 to 15 minutes, until golden
in color.

While allowing the buns to cool slightly, mix
together the powdered sugar, vanilla, remainder of the egg white and the dash of salt. You
want this frosting mixture to be of a piping
consistency (a soft paste or frosting-like con
sistency), so add more milk if necessary. Pipe
this mixture into the cross cut on top of the buns.

(If you do not have a pastry bag for piping
purposes, you can make a cone out of wax
paper, put the mixture in it so that there is
room at the top to close it and create a roll-
down from the top like a toothpaste tube. Snip
a small hole in the tip of the cone and squeeze
the frosting out by rolling down the top.)

Makes 18 buns.

From the files of Velma Post
Rushville, IL

Specialty Breads

Buttery Herb Rye Bread

1/2 cup (1 stick) butter
1 small clove garlic, crushed
1/4 t. basil
1/4 t. rosemary
1/4 t. thyme
1/4 t. orange peel, freshly grated
1/2 t. salt
1-1/2 cups orange juice, freshly squeezed
1 loaf rye bread

Preheat oven to 400°.

Combine softened butter with garlic, basil, rosemary, and thyme.

Add the orange juice, peel, and the salt. Mix well. Slice the bread in 1-inch slices down to, but not through, the bottom crust. Cut in half lengthwise, but not through the bottom crust. Spread the butter on all the cut surfaces. Wrap in foil, but do not cover the top. Heat for 10 to 12 minutes, until quite hot and lightly toasted on top.

Anonymous

Grape Nuts Bread

This was a war-time recipe passed down by my maternal grandmother. She probably added nuts to the recipe in "better times."

1 cup Post Grape Nuts
2 cups buttermilk
2 eggs
2 cups sugar
4 cups flour
1 t. baking soda
3 t. baking powder
1 t. salt
2 cups chopped nuts

Soak the Grape Nuts in the buttermilk until soft. Add the eggs and beat well. To this add the sugar, flour, baking soda, baking powder, salt, and chopped nuts.

Grease and flour two 4-1/2"x 2-1/2"x 8-1/2" loaf pans, and pour the batter into the pans.

Bake 1 hour in a slow oven (325°).

MAKES 2 LOAVES.

This sweet bread is a delicious addition to any holiday celebration and can stand alone or accompany cheese.

Cynthia Lang, Remedial Teacher
New York, NY

Hawk Circle's Hickory Nut Bread

Hickory nuts add a wonderfully mild, maple-like flavor to any traditional bread recipe.

Collecting the Hickory Nuts:

The collecting of the nuts in the fall, as well as the preparation for use, makes a great activity for kids! We gather our nuts in upstate New York between mid-October and mid-November from the Shagbark Hickory trees. You can collect the nuts both with and without the fleshy husk still on them. It is best to use the nuts within a few days of collecting them. If this is not possible, place the nuts in the refrigerator or freezer.

Determining Good Nuts from Bad Nuts:

It is important for this process to determine if the nuts are good or not and to eliminate the bad ones. This is done as follows: Fill a large soup pot to the top with cold water. After removing any fleshy husks, put the nuts into the pot. The bad nuts will float to the top, leaving the good nuts in the bottom of the pot.

Scoop out the highest floaters and discard. Select a few of the next highest floaters and crack open to check them. Usually the bad nut meat is dark brown to black in color. Place any good nuts in a bowl and discard the others. Repeat this process until you are confident that the remaining nuts are good. All of the nuts on the bottom will be good.

Hickory Cream:

1. "Grind" the Hickory nuts, shells and all.

There are a couple of ways that you can do this. Some of our students put the nuts in a high-walled, wooden box and pound them with a long, 6-foot pole (2 inches in diameter) held vertically. Some say the end of a baseball bat will work as well. I place the nuts in an old pillowcase and then in a cardboard box and pound them that way. To insure that the nuts are fully ground, both shells and nut meat, I open the pillowcase toward the end of my pounding, fold it over the sides of the box, and

pound again with the wooden pole to make sure they are really ground. The pillowcase is useful for keeping the pieces of shell from flying and hitting someone in the eye.

2. Make the Hickory Cream

Place the ground nuts, shells and all, into a large soup pot about three-quarteres full of water. Place on the stove and heat until just before it begins to boil. Remove from the burner immediately. Stir to loosen any nut meat that might be caught in the shells.

The nut meat, which is referred to as hickory cream, will now have all floated to the top and will appear as a thick, foamy layer on the surface of the water. Gently scoop the "cream" out and place into a bowl. [Note: you will want to use this in the bread recipe while it is still hot.] The water remaining in the pot is referred to as the hickory milk and may be used if the bread recipe needs extra water.

The Bread Recipe

2 pkgs. yeast
2 t. sugar
1/4 cup warm water
4 T. sugar
4 T. butter
1 T. salt
1 egg
2 cups hickory cream, hot
3 cups unbleached white flour
2-1/2 to 3 cups whole wheat flour

Combine the yeast and the 2 teaspoons sugar in a small bowl. Add the warm water and set aside until needed.

Combine the 4 tablespoons sugar, butter, and salt in a large bowl. Pour hickory cream, while still hot, over this mixture. Mix until the butter is melted. Let cool.

When cooled, add the egg and the yeast mixture. Then add the flours one cup at a time and stir after each addition. The dough will be easy to work with and to shape as desired.

Shape into a loaf, place in a bowl and cover with a warm, damp cloth. Set it aside in a warm place to rise.

Bake at 350° until firm and golden brown on the outside.

MAKES 1 LARGE LOAF THAT SERVES APPROXIMATELY 24 CHILDREN.

Suggestions: If you have extra hickory cream left over, blend it with a little maple syrup and honey to make a delicious spread for your warm bread! And left over hickory milk sweetened with a bit of maple syrup makes a yummy hot drink!

Luke Gailard & Trista Haggerty
Hawk Circle Wilderness Education
Cherry Valley, NY

Good Pizza Crust

2 t. yeast
1-2/3 cups warm water
1 T. honey or maple syrup
4 cups white flour
1 T. dried rosemary
2 t. salt

Combine yeast, water, and sweetener (honey or maple syrup). Let the mixture foam. Mix in flour, rosemary, and salt. Knead until you have a nice smooth ball. Let rise in a warm spot about an hour. Punch down and form two equal balls from the dough. Roll the balls out on a floured surface.

You are ready to put the toppings on.

Bake the pizza at 425° for 15 minutes or until done.

MAKES 2 10-INCH CRUSTS

Nancy Sky, Parent
Pleasant Ridge Waldorf School
Viroqua, WI

Breakfast Berry Shortcake

1 cup oats
1 cup pastry flour
1 T. baking powder
1/2 tsp. baking soda
1/4 cup butter
2/3 cup plain yogurt
2 cups yogurt and berries, mixed and sweetened

Preheat oven to 400°.

Lightly grease a cookie sheet.

Combine oats, flour, baking powder, and baking soda. Cut in butter until crumbly. Add the 2/3 cup yogurt; mix just until moistened. Knead on a floured surface 10 times. Place on a cookie sheet and form into an 8-inch circle.

Bake 15 to 20 minutes or until golden.

Serve warm. Cut into quarterse and spoon sweetened berries and yogurt over each piece.

Kelly Jansel, Former parent and secretary
Pleasant Ridge Waldorf School
Viroque, WI

Cheese Pretzels

1 T. dry active yeast
1 1/2 cups warm water
1 t. salt
1 tsp. sugar
3 cups whole-wheat flour
1-1/2 cups grated cheddar cheese
1 egg, beaten

Dissolve the yeast in warm water in a large bowl. Stir in salt and sugar. Add flour and cheese. Mix well. Knead dough on a floured surface until smooth. Cut off pieces and shape as desired. Place on an ungreased cookie sheet. Brush with beaten egg and sprinkle with sesame seeds, poppy seeds, or kosher salt.

Bake at 375° for 10 to 15 minutes.

Jean Young, Former parent
Pleasant Ridge Waldorf School
Viroqua, WI

Yummy Croutons

A great recipe for all those bread ends, leftover toast, etc. [Disclaimer . . . All of my recipes are measured according to taste, so taste away!]

olive oil
spices: I like garlic powder, cumin, a bit of thyme
bread ends, cubed

On medium heat (careful, these burn easily) throw the bread in with some olive oil. The oil disappears quickly, so have some extra to add as needed. The bread shouldn't be swimming in oil, but needs enough to not stick to the pan and to hold the spices. Cook and stir to evenly coat the bread. Add some spices, or not, as your mood and family dictate. Cook until somewhat browned — blackened is okay, it just adds character! Then add the croutons to your soups or salads and enjoy. They keep for a while in refrigerator if you have any leftovers!

Sarah Caldwell, Parent
Pleasant Ridge Waldorf School
Viroqua, WI

Muffins

Hearth in Hands Millet Muffins

1-1/2 cups flour
1/2 cup ground millet
1/4 cup honey
2 t. salt
1/4 t. nutmeg
1/2 t. cinnamon
1 cup applesauce
1/4 cup vegetable oil

Add all the dry ingredients in a bowl and mix. Add the applesauce and the oil and mix. (The children love grinding the millet in a coffee mill and rasping the nutmeg.)

Bake at 375° for 20 minutes.

MAKES 8 MUFFINS.

Yvonne deMaat
Hearth in Hand Bakery
Heart in Hand Preschool
Portland, OR

Oatmeal-Carrot Muffins

1 cup oats
2 cups whole wheat pastry flour
2 t. baking powder
1/4 t. salt
1 egg, lightly beaten
1/2 cup maple syrup
1 cup milk
1/4 cup vegetable oil
2 grated carrots
1 cup raisins
1 chopped pear (optional)

Preheat the oven to 400°.

In a large bowl, combine oats, flour, baking powder, and salt.

In a small bowl beat the egg and then add the maple syrup, milk, oil, and grated carrots. Mix well.

Pour the wet ingredients into the large bowl with the dry ingredients. Stir until just blended. Stir in the raisins and the (optional) chopped pear.

Divide the batter into 12 muffin cups, and bake for 20 to 25 minutes.

MAKES 12 MUFFINS.

Lisa Hildreth
Susquehanna Waldorf School
Marietta, PA

Awesome Blueberry Muffins

I'm always asked for recipes for the alternative baked goods I make, which I usually just throw together and rarely write down – this one was so good I did write it down. It contains no wheat, refined sugar, or dairy.

2 eggs
1/3 cup canola oil
1/3 cup Earth Balance Spread, melted
1 cup maple syrup
1-1/2 t. vanilla
2 T. grated fresh ginger root
2 cups rice milk

2 cups millet flour
1-1/2 cups spelt flour
1/2 cup buckwheat flour
1 cup flax meal (grind flax seeds in blender)
3 t. baking powder
1-1/2 t. baking soda
1 t. salt
2 t. cinnamon

2 cups fresh blueberries (otherwise, thawed frozen blueberries)

Blend eggs, oil, spread, syrup, vanilla, ginger root, and rice milk together with a whisk or beaters. Sift flours, meal, baking powder, soda, salt, and cinnamon together and mix gently with a spoon into the wet ingredients.

Add the blueberries and mix gently into the batter. Spoon the batter into muffin tins and bake at 350° for about 25 minutes, or until done.

MAKES 12 MUFFINS.

Rebecca Wainscott, Alumni Parent
Pleasant Ridge Waldorf School
Viroqua, WI

Blueberry Muffins

Dry ingredients:
3 cups unbleached organic white flour
1 cup whole wheat pastry flour
1/2 to 2 t. salt
2 T. baking powder

Wet ingredients:
1/2 cup corn oil
1/2 cup maple syrup
1/2 cup maple syrup
1/2 rice syrup
1/2 soymilk
1-1/2 cups apple juice
1 T. vanilla

1/2 pint blueberries

Preheat the oven to 325°.

Oil the muffin pans with corn oil or set paper muffin cups in the pan. In a large bowl, combine all the dry ingredients and mix well with a whisk. Set aside.

In a separate bowl, combine all the wet ingredients and mix well with a whisk. Pour the wet mixture into the dry mixture. Using a whisk, stir them just until mixed. Do not over mix. Add blueberries, stirring gently with a rubber spatula.

Fill the muffin cups, and bake for 50 minutes to 1 hour, or until the edges of the muffins are golden brown.

MAKES 12 MUFFINS.

Diane Prusha
Great Barrington Rudolf Steiner School
Great Barrington, MA

Quick Bran Muffins

1 box raisin bran cereal (15 oz. box)
3 cups sugar
5 cups flour
5 t. baking soda
2 tsp. Salt
5 to 6 t. cinnamon
4 eggs, beaten
1 cup butter, melted
1 qt. buttermilk

Mix raisin bran cereal, sugar, flour, baking soda, salt, and cinnamon in a large mixing bowl. Add eggs, butter, and buttermilk. Mix well. Fill muffin cups 2/3 full and bake for 15 to 20 minutes at 400°.

MAKES ABOUT 6 DOZEN MUFFINS.

Anonymous

Refrigerator Bran Muffins

3 cups bran
1 cups boiling water
1/2 cup light oil
1/2 to 3/4 cup honey
2 eggs
2-1/2 cups whole wheat flour
2-1/2 t. baking soda
2 cups buttermilk

Combine bran and boiled water in a large bowl. Stir and let steep. Mix oil, honey, and beaten eggs; add to bran mix. Mix flour and baking soda and add to bran mix alternately with the buttermilk. Refrigerate 12 hours before using. Can be used over the next couple of weeks from the refrigerator.

Add nuts, dates, raisins, and such, to the batter prior to baking.

Bake at 400° for 20 to 30 minutes.

Carole Austin, Parent
Pleasant Ridge Waldorf School
Viroqua, WI

Banana Muffins

Another quick and easy crowd pleaser…

2-1/2 ripe bananas
1 egg
2 T. honey
1-1/2 T. water
1/3 cup oil
1 t. vanilla
1-1/3 cups whole wheat pastry flour (I have used half barley flour with good results.)
2 t. baking powder
1/4 t. nutmeg

Mix bananas, egg, honey, water, oil, and vanilla. Sift together flour, powder, and nutmeg and add to the banana mixture. Mix. Spoon into oiled muffin tin. The cups should be about 2/3 full.

Bake at 350° for 30 minutes. Let cool a bit before devouring!

Nancy Sky, Parent
Pleasant Ridge Waldorf School
Viroqua, WI

Honey Muffins

(Contains no eggs or dairy!)

2-1/2 cups flour
1/2 cup honey or maple syrup
2 t. vanilla
1 cup milk alternative (soy, rice, etc.)
1/4 cup oil
2 t. baking powder
Pinch of salt

Preheat oven to 350°. Oil the muffin pan.

Mix all ingredients until just blended. Bake for 30 minutes.

Ruth Kasl, Kindergarten Teacher
Susquehanna Waldorf School
Marietta, PA

Cran-Apple Walnut Muffins

These are not too sweet and very satisfying. They're also dairy-free.

1 cup sugar
1/2 cup vegetable oil
2 eggs
1 tsp. vanilla
2 1/4 cups whole wheat flour
1 tsp. soda
2 tsp. cinnamon
1 tsp. nutmeg
2 cups sliced apples
1/2 lb. whole raw cranberries (1 cup)
or 3 cups sliced apples
or 3 cups chopped rhubarb
1/2 cup chopped walnuts

Cream sugar and oil together. Add eggs and vanilla and beat until fluffy. In a separate bowl mix flour, soda, cinnamon, and nutmeg. To the flour mixture add fruit and nuts.

Pour liquid into dry mix and mix a few quick strokes. Bake at 350° for 45 to 50 minutes.

Geri Shonka, Parent
Pleasant Ridge Waldorf School
Viroqua, WI

Zucchini Muffins

1/2 cup sugar
1 large egg, lightly beaten
1/4 cup vegetable oil
3/4 cup all-purpose flour
1/4 t. baking powder
1/4 t. baking soda
1/4 t. salt
1/4 t. freshly grated nutmeg
1 cup grated zucchini (about 1/4 pound)
1/4 cup raisins, finely chopped
1/4 cup chopped pecans

Preheat oven to 350°. Combine sugar, egg, and oil in a large bowl. Mix well.

Sift the flour with the baking powder, baking soda, salt, and nutmeg. Stir this into the egg mixture.

Add zucchini, raisins, and pecans. Stir only until blended.

Spoon batter into a well-buttered muffin tin, filling each cup about 2/3 full. Bake until golden brown, and toothpick comes out clean (about 25 minutes).

MAKES 9 MUFFINS.

Lynn Fitzgerald
Table Grove, IL

Rolls, Buns, Biscuits & Scones

Onion Rolls

2 T. sugar
1 pkg. active dry yeast
2 t. salt
5 to 5-1/2 cups flour
2 cups milk
1/4 cup butter
3/4 cup chopped onion
Melted butter
Cornmeal
Paprika

Preheat the oven to 400°.

Combine the sugar, yeast, salt, and 2 cups of the flour in a large mixing bowl.

Heat together the milk and butter until very warm (120° to 130°). Gradually add this mixture to the dry ingredients and beat 2 minutes at medium speed of a mixer. Scrape the bowl occasionally. Add 1 cup of flour and beat 2 minutes at high speed, still scraping the sides of the bowl occasionally. Stir in 1/4 cup of the onions and enough additional flour to make a stiff dough.

Turn out onto a lightly floured surface and knead it until smooth and elastic (approximately 5 to 10 minutes). Place in a buttered bowl. Butter the top. Cover and let it rise in a warm place until it doubles in size (about 1 hour). Punch the dough down.

Divide the dough into 20 pieces, shaping them into balls and flattening them slightly. Place the balls about 3 inches apart on buttered baking sheets that have been sprinkled with cornmeal. Cover them, and let them rise in a warm place until they double in size (about 30 to 45 minutes). Brush the top of the rolls with melted butter. Sprinkle them with the remaining onion and then paprika.

Bake 18 to 20 minutes.

MAKES 20 ROLLS.

Anonymous

Rolls

2 T. honey
3 cups warm water
2 T. yeast
3 T. oil
8 cups flour (your choice)

Stir together the honey, warm water, and yeast. Wait for it to get foamy. Add the oil and flour, a cup at a time. Stir until it forms a

dough. Knead the dough and form into rolls. Let rise about 30 minutes.

Bake at 325° for about 18 minutes.

Ruth Kasl, Kindergarten Teacher
Susquehanna Waldorf School
Marietta, PA

Tal's Brown Oatmeal Rolls

2 cups boiling water
1 cup oatmeal
3 T. salad oil or shortening (melted butter)
1 package yeast
1/3 cup lukewarm water
2/3 cup brown sugar
2 t. salt
5 to 5-1/2 cups flour

Pour boiling water over oats, cool to lukewarm. Add salad oil, yeast softened in water,
brown sugar, and salt. Beat in flour to make a
soft dough. Knead. Let rise until doubled.

Punch down and let rise again.

Roll dough 1/2 inch thick, and cut into any
desired shape.
Let rise until doubled.

Bake at 375° for 20 to 25 minutes.

Adding cereals to breads is a great way to
"start" bread. Cooking the grain and then
adding the flour creates a natural "sponge"
that is ripe for the yeast.

Note: Be careful to allow cooling time when
you add boiling water to the grain before you
add the yeast. If the mixture is too hot it will
kill the yeast. Often "grain" breads will start
out sticky and may require extra kneading
time, but this dough makes delicious bread.

From the kitchen of my husband's grandmother, this was probably a recipe from war
time when flour was scarce and cooks used
other, less expensive, grains to conserve their
supplies.

MAKES 3 TO 4 DOZEN.

Cynthia Lang, Remedial Teacher
New York, NY

Butter Horns

3/4 cup milk, scalded
1/2 cup butter (1 stick)
1/2 cup sugar
1/2 t. salt
2 cakes yeast
3 eggs, beaten
4-1/2 cups flour (or 4 to 4-1/2)

Combine milk, butter, sugar, and salt. Let it
cool until lukewarm. Add the yeast and stir
well, without dissolving the yeast. Add the
beaten eggs and flour to form the dough.

Place the dough in a lightly greased bowl,
cover, and let it rise until double in size. Divide
the dough into three pieces and roll each into
a 9-inch circle, and 1/4 inch thick. Cut each
circle into 12 wedges. Brush these with melted
butter.

Starting at the wide end, roll each wedge into
a horn. Place on a greased baking pan, brush
with melted butter, and let rise.

Bake on the lower rack at 375° for 10 to 15
minutes (watch carefully).

MAKES 36 HORNS.

Betty Johnson
Rushville, IL

Refrigerator Rolls with Potatoes

6 to 8 cups sifted flour
1 t. salt
1/2 cup sugar
2 eggs
1 cup sweet milk (scalded and cooled to lukewarm)
1 cake compressed yeast dissolved in 1/2 cup lukewarm water
2/3 cup shortening, softened (your choice)
1 cup mashed potatoes

Put flour, salt, and sugar into bowl. Beat eggs, add cooled milk, water, yeast, shortening, and mashed potatoes. Beat well and add to dry ingredients. Mix well. Knead until the ingredients are well distributed. Set in a warm place and let the dough rise until double in bulk. Punch it down and put into the refrigerator immediately. About an hour before you wish to bake the rolls, take the dough from the refrigerator and make into rolls. Let rise again until double in size.

Bake at 400° for 20 minutes.

From the files of
Velma Post
Rushville, IL

Kindergarten Buns

These are the buns that the kindergarteners in the Rosemary Kindergarten make every Tuesday to eat with their soup.

1/8 cup yeast
1/4 cup honey
3 cups warm water
3-1/2 cups whole wheat flour
3-1/2 cups white flour
1/4 cup oil
1 T. salt

Add yeast and honey to water and whisk together. Add 2 cups whole wheat flour and 2 cups white flour. Stir for 100 strokes. Cover with a damp towel and let sit for 1 hour, or until doubled. Add oil and salt. Fold together. Add 1-1/2 cups each of the whole wheat flour and white flour. Fold in and then knead the dough about 15 minutes. Knead in up to 1 more cup of flour, if needed, to keep dough from being too sticky. Form into buns (about 24). Place on cornmeal-sprinkled cookie sheet. Leave some space between them. Bake about 20 minutes at 350°, or until lightly browned.

Anne-Marie Fryer, Kindergarten teacher
Pleasant Ridge Waldorf School
Viroqua, WI

Raisin Scones

5 cups all-purpose flour (sometimes I use half whole wheat and half white flour.)
1 T. baking powder
1/4 T. baking soda
1 t. salt
1/2 cup sugar
1 cup butter
1-1/2 cups buttermilk – add in thirds
1 cup raisins
(add any spices you like such as cinnamon, nutmeg, allspice)

Blend dry ingredients. Quickly cut in butter. Make a well in the center. Add buttermilk and raisins just until combined. Do not over mix. Gather dough. Form into an 8-inch round on a floured counter. Do not flatten too much. Cut into wedges. Place on a non-stick baking sheet. Bake at 400° for 15 to 20 minutes. Cool. Serve with jam and butter.

Kay Fandel, Parent
Pleasant Ridge Waldorf School
Viroqua, WI

41

Currant Scones

1 cup unsalted butter
About 4 cups unbleached, all-purpose flour
1/2 cup sugar
2 t. baking powder
1/2 t. baking soda
1/4 t. salt
2 cups heavy cream
1 cup currants

Line 2 cookie sheets with parchment.

Preheat oven to 400° at least 20 minutes before baking. Set an oven rack at the middle level before preheating.

Cut the butter into 1-inch cubes and refrigerate them for at least 30 minutes or freeze them for 10 minutes.

In a large bowl, whisk together the flour, sugar, baking powder, baking soda, and salt. Add the butter and, with your fingertips, press the cubes into large flakes. Mix in the cream just until the flour is moistened and the dough starts to come together in large clumps. Mix in the currents. Knead the dough in the bowl just until it holds together and turn it out onto a lightly floured board.

Lightly flour the top of the dough, or use a rolling pin with a floured pastry sleeve, and roll out the dough into a rectangle 1 inch thick and about 8 by 12 inches. Use a scraper to keep the edge even. Fold the dough in thirds, like a business letter. Lightly flour the board and rotate the dough so that the smooth side faces to the left. Roll it out again to an 8"x12" rectangle and repeat the "turn" 3 times (for a total of 4 turns.) Refrigerate the dough, covered with plastic wrap, for about 15 minutes if it begins to soften and stick.

Roll out the dough once more and trim off the folded edges so that it will rise evenly. Cut it lengthwise in half so you have 2 pieces, each about 4 x 12 inches. Cut each piece of dough on the diagonal to form triangles with about a 3-inch wide base and place them about 1 inch apart on the prepared cookie sheets.

Bake the scones for 15 to 20 minutes, or until the edges begin to brown and the tops are golden brown and firm enough so that they barely give when pressed lightly with a finger.

Check scones after 10 minutes of baking, and if they are not baking evenly, rotate the cookie sheets from top to bottom and front to back. Do not over-bake, as the scones continue baking slightly after removal from the oven and are best when slightly moist and soft inside.

Place a linen towel on each of two large racks and place the baked scones on top. Fold the towels over loosely and allow the scones to cool until warm, or room temperature. (Since linen breathes, the scones will not become soggy, but they will have enough protection to keep from becoming dry and hard on the surface.)

Fernando and Marian León
Ann Arbor, MI

Hazelnut and Golden Raisin Scones

5 cups all-purpose flour
1 T. baking powder
1/4 T. baking soda
1 t. salt
1/2 cup sugar
1 cup butter
1-1/4 cups buttermilk – add in thirds
1 cup golden raisins
1/2 cup toasted hazelnuts

Blend dry ingredients. Quickly cut in butter. Make a well in the center and add buttermilk, nuts, and raisins, just until combined. Do not over mix. Gather dough. Form into an 8 inch round, on a floured counter. Do not flatten too much. Cut into wedges. Place on non-stick baking sheet. Bake at 400° for 15 to 20 minutes. Cool. Serve with jam and butter.

Kay Fandel, Parent
Pleasant Ridge Waldorf School
Viroqua, WI

Cheese Scones

2 cups bread flour
1 tablespoon sugar
2 t. baking powder
1/2 t. salt
1 packed cup grated cheddar cheese
3/4 cup (or more) chilled whole milk
1 egg
1 tablespoon vegetable oil

Preheat oven to 450°F.

Whisk flour, sugar, baking powder, and salt in a large bowl. Stir in cheese. Whisk milk, egg, and oil in a small bowl. Gradually add the milk mixture to the dry ingredients.

Turn the dough out onto a lightly floured surface; knead just until the dough is firm and consistent.

Pat out the dough to a 1-inch-thick round and cut into wedges. Bake 10 to 15 minutes, until golden. Serve warm.

Anonymous

Sky High Biscuits

2 cups white flour
1 cup whole wheat flour
4-1/2 t. baking powder
2 T. sugar
1/2 t. salt
3/4 t. cream of tartar
3/4 cup butter
1 egg, beaten
1 cup milk

Combine the flours, baking powder, sugar, salt, and cream of tartar. Cut in the butter until the mixture resembles coarse oatmeal. Add the egg and milk, stirring quickly. Knead the dough lightly on a floured board. Roll or pat gently to one inch thickness. Cut it into biscuits 1 to 2 inches in size. Place in a 10-inch skillet or a 9-inch square pan. (For crusty biscuits, separate them on a cookie sheet.)

Bake at 450° for 12 to 15 minutes.

Anonymous

Summer Flower Fairy Biscuits

Four-to-six-year-old children love to ask the flower fairies if they may pick their flowers. The children can look inside the petals and gently remove the little insects, too. Tearing the flower petals into tiny pieces is good for their growing fingers. Soaking the flowers makes the nutrients of the grain more available. Be kind to yourself, and make a double batch.

3-1/2 cups freshly ground spelt, kamut, or whole wheat flour
1 cup buttermilk
4 T. melted butter
1-1/2 t. sea salt
2 t. baking soda
extra flour for kneading
2 each orange and yellow daylily flowers
4 red bee balm flowers, petals only
4 sprigs parsley

Mix the flour with buttermilk to form a thick dough. Cover and leave in a warm place for 12 to 24 hours.

Place in a food processor and process several minutes to knead, or knead with well-floured hands.

Tear daylily flowers and parsley into tiny pieces; add the bee balm petals. Combine with flour, melted butter, salt, and baking soda. Knead dough and turn out onto a well-floured pastry cloth or board. Sprinkle with additional flour to prevent sticking. Flatten the dough to about 3/4 inch thickness and cut into rounds with a glass. Place on a buttered baking sheet.

Bake at 350° for 35 to 45 minutes.

Shannon Landis, Teacher and Alumni Parent
Pleasant Ridge Waldorf School
Viroqua, WI

Popovers & Puffs

Clopper's Poppers

2/3 cup whole wheat flour
1/3 cup white flour
1 cup milk
4 eggs
1/2 t. salt
2 T. melted butter
1 t. to 1 T. honey (optional)

Preheat oven to 425°. Grease popover tin or muffin tin and place in oven to preheat.

Combine all the ingredients, mixing them well. Do not over beat.

Pull the tin out of the oven and fill the cups 3/4 full. (Overfilling will make them more like muffins.) Return the pan to the oven. After 15 minutes reduce the temperature to 375° for another 15 minutes.

Be ready to eat them as soon as they come out of the oven. They are most glorious at that moment. Two minutes later they begin to fall.

Clopper Almon
Silver Springs, MD

Rosemary Popovers

2 eggs
1 cup milk
2 T. melted butter
l cup sifted flour
1/4 t. sea salt
2 T. rosemary, chopped fine

Preheat oven to 425°.

Butter the pan. Combine eggs, milk, and salt and wisk lightly. Stir in butter. Add flour and rosemary and mix until just blended. Do not overbeat. Fill each cup about half full.

Bake at 425° for 20 minutes. Reduce heat to 350° for 10 to 12 minutes, or until popovers are crisp and golden on the outside. Serve immediately.

Makes 6 large popovers in a popover pan, or 12 smaller ones in a standard muffin pan.

Gloria Kemp, Retired Teacher
Hawthorne Valley School, Harlemville, NY
Rudolf Steiner School, New York City

Susan's Puffs

1 T. yeast
1/4 cup warm water
1 cup cottage cheese
1 t. salt
2 T. brown sugar
1 egg
1 T. butter
2 t. poppy seeds
Lemon peel, grated
2-1/4 cups flour

Add yeast to the water. Melt the butter. Mix in cottage cheese, salt, and sugar. Heat to warm.

Add the mixture to the yeast. Add egg, poppy seeds, lemon peel, and 1-1/4 cups flour. Knead in the remaining cup of flour. Let rise in a bowl. Divide into 12 balls. Let rise again.

Bake at 400° for 15 minutes. They rise quickly.

(You can also use yogurt or sour cream instead of cottage cheese in this recipe.)

Sherry Knapp, Former parent
Pleasant Ridge Waldorf School
Viroqua, WI

Sourdough Breads

Sourdough is made with a wild yeast starter as opposed to commercial dried yeast. Basically, you mix flour and water and leave this mixture exposed to the air. Do use organic (preferably bio-dynamic) grains to get the best nourishment you can. What "starts" the bread, turning it from inert flour and water into an active, bubbling mix, is the development of a healthy culture of lactobacilli, a wild, airborne yeast.

Really all that is required to make your own starter is the best flour you can find. After a few days, without any disturbances, the mixture begins to ferment as the wild airborne yeast and friendly bacteria and make the bread rise and become established. Each starter is subtly different, which is what gives this bread its distinctive character and flavor.

If you bake fairly frequently, divide and feed your starter, using flour and water, once a day. If you aren't going to bake for a while, you can keep it dormant in the refrigerator for several months.

The original leavened bread was sourdough bread made from rye (but it also works with wheat). Sourdough is the end product of a process in which we take guiding control over spontaneous fermentation, a phenomenon which naturally occurs in a mixture of grain flour and water. This fermentation is caused by microbes — especially lactic acid bacteria and yeast fungi — which create an acid condition and generate gases, mostly in the form of carbon dioxide. The first provides the distinctive aroma, the latter the leavening and characteristic texture of the bread. To our senses the dough has a slightly sour smell and flavor, hence the name.

The procedure of making the dough is fairly simple. Besides the ingredients of flour and water, it requires a slightly warmed environment, some human intervention, and most importantly, resting periods during which the airy and aromatic elementals can render their service and perform the necessary transformation of the grain. With rye it takes normally five risings until the dough is fully developed. After that the fermentation needs to be brought to a halt by baking the dough in an oven. (Before the baking some dough is saved to be used as starter in the next batch, avoiding the necessity of starting from scratch when making new dough.) Under the high temperature in the oven the fermentation will end and the form of the bread stabilize.

Out of the oven comes something totally different: a deliciously fragrant loaf of bread! Made from whole grain, augmented through the process, eaten in joy, it has provided us with the opportunity to make full use of our capacities. Sourdough bread is the archetype and, at the same time, a fulfilling food for human nourishment.

Wolfgang Rohrs
Albany, NY

Mother Dough, Whole Wheat Sourdough Starter

If you are taking good care of the starter, it will get stronger and last for a long time. In Denmark I had a mother dough more than 100 years old passed down through generations.

1 cup freshly ground whole wheat flour
1 cup water
1/4 cup water (each day for 6 days)
1/4 cup whole wheat flour (each day for 6 days)

Mix 1 cup flour and 1 cup water in a glass bowl or jar. (Use a wooden spoon, always.) Cover with a cotton cloth and place in a cool place or outside in a shaded area.

Everyday for the next 6 days transfer the mother dough to a new clean bowl or jar. Feed the starter with 1 cup water and 1 cup flour, cover with a cloth and return it to the cool place.

Place this mother dough in the refrigerator, until you are ready to use it. Use a jar with a lid that allows the mother dough to breathe. If you leave the mother dough longer than one week, feed it again as described above and put it back in the refrigerator.

Keep 3 cups mother dough in the refrigerator at all times, if you want to be able to spontaneously bake any day. Otherwise, just keep 1 cup mother dough and the day before you want to bake, feed the mother dough with enough flour and water to make 3 cups—2 cups for the bread and 1 cup to keep for next time. The mother dough is always kept separate from the bread dough.

Anne-Marie Fryer, Teacher
Pleasant Ridge Waldorf School
Viroqua, WI

Kid Tested Sourdough Bread

To begin with you need to obtain a starter. You can get it from a friend, make your own, or buy a starter kit at a health food store.

The Previous Night:
Take your starter (1/2 cup) out of the refrigerator and let it come to room temperature (about an hour).

If there is a layer of strong-smelling greenish/bluish liquid on top, pour it off. This happens when you do not use your starter often. It has a high alcohol content and early pioneers would drink it "in a pinch."

Add 2 cups of warm water (85°) to the starter and mix in enough unbleached flour (about 2-1/2 cups) until you get a thick consistency.

Leave it in a warm place overnight (70 to 80°). The oven with the pilot light on works well.

Baking Day:
Your starter should look pretty cheery and bubbly. If not, set it in a warmer place until it is ready.

IMPORTANT: Take out 1/2 cup of the starter for the next time you bake!

With the remaining sponge (as it is now called) add as much flour as you need to get a good dough consistency. I use equal amounts of unbleached and whole wheat flour. Toward the end of the mixing, add 1 T. salt.

Make sure it is not too sticky before turning it out onto a counter sprinkled with flour. Start kneading it, adding small amounts of flour at a time. In time, you will get a feel for how much flour you need to use. The dough should not stick anymore, but also should not absorb too much flour.

Divide the dough and place in loaf pans. Let rise in a warm room for 3 to 4 hours until the dough has doubled in size.

Preheat the oven to 450°. Place the loaves in the oven, lower the temperature to 400°, and bake until brown.

MAKES 2 LOAVES.

Yvonne deMaat
Hearth in Hand Bakery
Heart in Hand Preschool
Portland, OR

Sourdough Bread

I serve sourdough bread to the children in my two-day Sunrise Garden class, which is a transitional program from Parent/Child to an Early Childhood style class. I do not measure out the ingredients so the recipe is roughly as follows:

4 cups sourdough starter
1 T. salt
1 cup sesame seeds or course ground grain
3+ cups organic whole wheat flour
3+ cups organic white flour

Pour starter into a large mixing bowl, while reserving at least 1 cup for next week's bread dough. Mix in salt and sesame seeds and then slowly stir in the flour. Toward the end it will be easier to knead it with your hands. If the

dough becomes too dry add water; it should be soft and easy to work. Knead and add flour until it is just no longer sticky. I let it rise and then refrigerate it until the next morning.

The next morning bring the dough to room temperature again and let the children form shapes/rolls.

Bake at 375° to 400° for 30 to 40 minutes, or until browned.

If the dough is formed into a loaf a longer baking time of approximately 1 hour will be needed.

Starter came be used repeatedly once it is established. A good recipe for starter can be found on p. 48 and also in Sally Fallon's *Nourishing Traditions*. To build up enough starter I mix in a cup of either organic whole wheat or white flour each day and enough good filtered water to form a pancake batter consistency. I leave the starter in a loosely covered jar or bowl to bubble and froth at room temperature.

MAKES 18 ROLLS OR 2 LOAVES.

Karen Hays, Early Childhood Educator
Four Winds Waldorf School
Warrenville, IL

Whole Wheat Sourdough Bread

3 cups mother dough or starter
1 cup water
1 T. sea salt
1 T. barley malt (optional)
4 to 5 cups whole wheat flour or half unbleached white flour

Place 2 cups of the mother dough in a large mixing bowl. Place 1 cup in a pint size jar in the refrigerator for your next bread making. Add water, salt, and barley malt to the 2 cups of mother dough in the bowl. Mix it very well with a wooden spoon. If you want to add raisins and cinnamon, this is the time.

Add the flour a little at a time. Sift the un-bleached flour. Use clean hands to form a moist light dough the consistency of an ear lobe. The amount of flour varies, dependent on the variety and moisture in the flour. If too much flour is added the dough becomes hard.

Knead the dough in the bowl rhythmically for a few minutes. Cover with a moist, cotton cloth and leave it to rise in a warm place for 1 to 3 hours. (An oven with a pilot light works well.) The rising time varies, depending on the time of day, the phase of the moon, the season, and the temperature of the room. Over-rising makes the bread too sour.

Oil a bread pan with sesame oil. Moisten your hands. Knead the dough again gently for a minute. Place the dough in the bread pan. The dough should fill the pan about one half to two-thirds up from the bottom. Let it rise again under a moist, cotton cloth in a warm place for 2 to 6 hours, or until almost double in size.

Preheat the oven to 350° and place the bread on the top shelf.

Bake for 40 to 60 minutes, or until golden. The bread will sound hollow when it is tapped. Remove the bread from the pan and let cool on an oven rack or wire before slicing.

Well-done sourdough bread is sweet and only slightly sour. Store bread wrapped in paper, inside a plastic bag in a cool place. It keeps well for 6 to 10 days. Week-old bread can be sliced and reheated, toasted, or steamed before serving.

MAKES 2 LOAVES.

Anne-Marie Fryer, Teacher
Pleasant Ridge Waldorf School
Viroqua, WI

Honey-Salt-Bread: A Bread for Our Time

The honey-salt process uses honey to initiate the spontaneous fermentation of the dough. After the third rising, salt is applied as a balance. The special effect is that the nectar yeasts, which are naturally to be found on the blossoms of the flowers, are the driving force in the leavening. They get picked up by the bees while collecting the nectar and are then carried into the honey.

I have baked honey-salt-bread for the last two years successfully with rye and blends of rye and spelt. The results were always very satisfying. The characteristics of these breads are: a lovely aroma; a full bodied but mild flavor; a dense, moist, chewy texture (requiring just the right amount of chewing time to mix properly with the enzymes in the mouth); very acceptable to the stomach; conducive to digestion; substantive; delicious with any kind of spread; lasting in storage. It pleases the palate as well as the metabolic system. I became so enthusiastic about honey-salt-bread that I now bake it for my own use on a regular basis. I prefer to use the baking ferment (it provides a very mild bread), but also work from scratch according to the following recipe.

The honey-salt-bread seems to be a bread for our time. First of all, it is so well adaptable to the highly stressed metabolism of modern people, easing the condition of mental activity. We need a clear head to develop the faculties of imagination, inspiration, and intuition. The acquisition of these new abilities demands balance and groundedness, with which the airy element in leavened bread might interfere, leading one to illusion. This risk will be less with the honey-salt-bread which exhibits a denser texture, indicating less penetration of the air element. But even here, moderation of consumption seems to be advisable.

Recipe for Honey-Salt-Bread

This recipe is based on my own experiences during which I worked with indications by Maria Thun from her book Work on the Land and the Constellations.

Start in the evening:
Dissolve 2 T. of raw wildflower honey in 1/2 cup of 100° water; mix in 1 cup of fine rye flour (or a blend of rye and spelt. You can also use whole wheat flour). Cover well (e.g., with a damp towel and plate on top of bowl) so the mixture does not dry out. Let sit overnight and keep warm between 85° and 90° (e.g., near the stove or inside an oven with only the light on).

Next morning:
Some bubbles should be noticeable. Add the same amounts of warm water and flour and mix in well.

In the evening:
Add 5 cups of flour (ground to the coarseness of your liking) and 2 cups of 100° water to the above mixture. Stir in well. Let mixture rise in the same warm and covered condition.

Next morning:
Add to the risen dough 3 cups of flour and 1/3 cup of 140° water in which 2-1/2 t. of salt is dissolved. Knead the mixture well for not more than ten minutes into a smooth dough. You might add flax seeds, and caraway, fennel, or anise seeds, and ground coriander or cardamom, according to your taste. Let the dough rise well for at least one hour while keeping it warm at 95°, covering well against loss of moisture. (You can now put aside 1 cup of the dough as "starter" to eliminate the first two risings in your next batch. For the new batch dissolve the withheld starter with 1 t. of honey in the water before mixing in the fluid. Store the starter in a cold place).

Form the dough into a loaf, place on a greased baking sheet or in a baking pan, and let it rise well again for around 1 hour, in the same warm and covered condition. (If the dough starts to shrink, it was too long, and it must be re-formed.) Bake in a preheated oven at 375° for about 1 hour. In order to have a softer crust you might bake at a lower temperature for a longer period. For example, start with 200° for 30 minutes, then 250° for 15 minutes, then 300° for 15 minutes, then 350° for 30 minutes.

For moisture during baking put a container with a cupful of water at the bottom of the oven. After baking, place on a grate to cool; store the loaf wrapped in a paper bag in a bread drawer. Allow a couple of days before eating. Cover the sliced end with waxed paper to maintain freshness.

Some additional notes:
One is often tempted to experiment further with something good, and so it was that I tried some other applications for this delicious, nourishing dough. Starting with a German fruit bread, which turned out to be rich and very desirable for autumn and winter festivals, I then used it as a pizza dough with a number of seasonal toppings. The results were tasty, wholesome pizza such as I had never eaten before. A waffle recipe was also successful.

Fruit and Nut Bread
Using the basic honey-salt bread recipe, add cinnamon, nutmeg, ground cloves, whole dried figs, prunes (pitted), apricots, and lightly toasted filberts/hazelnuts to the risen dough on the second morning after the last addition of flour and water. Knead into the dough mixture. Continue as described in the recipe. This fruit and nut bread is delicious simply as is or spread with butter, if you wish.

Pizza
What a way to bring nourishing rye and veggies to teenagers! Usually we double the basic honey-salt recipe, which is enough to make two pizza crusts. We either store the pizza dough tightly covered in the refrigerator until ready to use within a couple of days or pat and roll the dough into 3/16" thickness on an

oiled pizza pan. Allow to rise for one hour in a warm and covered condition. Meanwhile prepare topping. Seasonal variations include chopped kale or spinach tossed with thyme or dill, and a sprinkling of herb salt and oil to coat. Cover dough with the greens; top with thinly sliced onions or leek, also tossed with herbs and oil if no cheese is used. Top the pizza with either sunflower or sesame seeds and mozzarella cheese or tofu blended with herbs, oil, and herb salt. A circle of sesame-oiled, grated red beets or carrots are tasty additions.

Bake at 400° for 20 minutes or until the bottom and edges are golden brown.

Waffles

To one cup of honey-salt dough, add 4 cups of flour and 1-1/2 cups of milk (low-fat or soy) in a large bowl. Allow to stand covered in a warm place overnight or from morning to evening. Lightly mix 2 to 3 T. carbonated mineral water and 1/4 t. salt into the batter just before use. Bake waffles on lightly oiled, heated waffle iron for 5 to 7 minutes. Finely chopped pecan bits, grated coconut, or berries in season can be added to the batter before baking. Waffles can be kept warm in 200° oven until ready for serving.

Wolfgang Rohrs
Albany, NY

Index

Marsha Post is senior editor, translator, and Waldorf and adult education coordinator for SteinerBooks. While living in New York City, she was a leader in the Anthroposophical Society branch, and she has served on the General Council of the Anthroposophical Society.

Jo Valens is a Waldorf Teacher who lives with her husband in Great Barrington, Massachusetts. Jo fills her empty-nest hours with drawing, gardening, walking, and conversing with friends and strangers.

The author of six novels and many magazine articles, **Winslow Eliot** worked in publishing in New York City for twenty years before moving to the Berkshires with her family. She is a Waldorf teacher and the mother of two Waldorf graduates. She lives with her husband in Alford, Massachusetts.